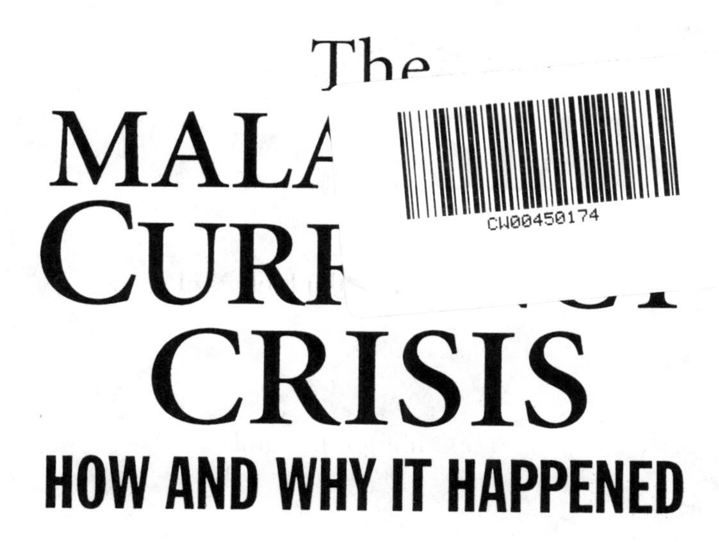

HOW AND WHY IT HAPPENED

Mahathir Mohamad

Pelanduk
Publications
www.pelanduk.com

Published by
Pelanduk Publications (M) Sdn Bhd
(Co. No. 113307-W)
12 Jalan SS13/3E
Subang Jaya Industrial Estate
47500 Subang Jaya
Selangor Darul Ehsan, Malaysia

Address all correspondence to
Pelanduk Publications (M) Sdn Bhd
P.O. Box 8265, 46785 Kelana Jaya
Selangor Darul Ehsan, Malaysia

Check out our website at *www.pelanduk.com*
e-mail: *mypp@tm.net.my*

Perpustakaan Negara Malaysia   Cataloguing-in-Publication Data

Mahathir bin Mohamad, Dato' Seri, 1925-
The Malaysian currency crisis / Mahathir Mohamad.
Includes index
ISBN 967-978-756-7
1. Foreign exchange—Malaysia. 2. Financial crises—Malaysia. 3. Malaysia—Economic conditions. I. Title.
332.4509595

Printed and bound in Malaysia

The MALAYSIAN CURRENCY CRISIS

£2

39L

Books by Dr Mahathir Mohamad

The Malaysian Currency Crisis
A New Deal for Asia
The Way Forward
The Challenges of Turmoil
The Voice of Asia: Two Leaders Discuss the Coming Century (with Shintaro Ishihara)
The Challenge
The Malay Dilemma

CONTENTS

PREFACE

FOR ten consecutive years, Malaysia, a multiracial country which had always believed in the free market, grew by 8 per cent plus annually. It had always been politically stable and economically resilient. Its currency was strong and its international debts were well within accepted limits. Indeed, it was able to prepay loans repeatedly. It was certainly not a candidate for severe recession. A slowdown in growth perhaps, but not economic and financial turmoil.

Yet in July 1997, its currency began to devalue rapidly and its stock market plunged to extremely low levels. The pundits aver that this sudden downturn was due to bad governance and the contagion effect of the fall of the Thai baht. The fall in the value of the ringgit and stock-market capitalisation looked likely to be continuous and could not be arrested. Malaysians were bewildered as they found themselves suddenly impoverished.

The country and the government were completely unprepared to deal with the seriously deteriorating economy. But government leaders quickly identified currency traders and short-term investors as the culprits responsible for the turmoil. But knowing who were responsible for the turmoil was not enough. It was necessary to understand how they operated and how to counter their attacks on the Malaysian economy.

It is my sincere hope that in detailing the country's experience in handling the economic and financial turmoil, Malaysians will understand the very serious difficulty the country was in and appreciate the measures taken by the government to overcome the turmoil. It is also hoped that Malaysia's experience will provide invaluable lessons to other countries which might face similar situations.

DR MAHATHIR BIN MOHAMAD
PUTRAJAYA
August 29, 2000

1.
STRONG ECONOMIC FUNDAMENTALS

WHEN the Malaysian ringgit came under speculative attack in July 1997, the Malaysian government was totally unprepared to deal with the turmoil which ensued. No one seemed to understand what was happening and why the ringgit was depreciating so rapidly against the US dollar. For a long time the ringgit had been trading at around 2.50 against the US dollar and the trading range was narrow and reasonable.

The ringgit was considered a strong and stable currency. Some, in fact, felt that it was slightly undervalued. The government did not officially peg the ringgit to the US dollar. The rate of 2.50 per US dollar and the narrow trading range around it were determined apparently by the market. Any volatility in the exchange rate was easily moderated by Bank Negara Malaysia (the Malaysian central bank) through minimal intervention and such interventions were few and far between. The Malaysian government had always believed in the importance of stability in all sectors, and the ringgit exchange rate was no exception. Stability is vital for development and growth and for the business sector to manage their businesses successfully. The government wants to see businesses profitable because it has a 28 per cent stake in the profits made through corporate tax.

The ringgit's exchange rate was also generally stable against regional currencies. Against the currencies of two of Malaysia's neighbours, Thailand and the Philippines, the ringgit was stable at 1 ringgit to 10 Thai baht and 1 ringgit to 10 Philippine peso. The ringgit did appreciate against the Indonesian rupiah but this was due to the rupiah's weakness against most currencies, including the ringgit.

The Thai baht, unlike the ringgit, was fixed by the Thai government at about 25 baht against the US dollar. Since the baht rate against the ringgit was steady at 10, there was a wrong perception amongst some that the ringgit was also pegged against the US dollar at 2.50.

On the back of the currency stability (at 2.50 against the US dollar) Malaysia was doing very well. At the end of 1996, real Gross Domestic Product (GDP) grew at almost 8.5 per cent per annum for ten consecutive years and it looked like this rate of growth was going to continue for many more years. By 1997 total external trade reached more than US$158 billion, making Malaysia according to the World Trade Organisation (WTO), the 18th biggest exporting nation and the 17th biggest importing nation in the world. The government was enjoying a fiscal surplus. The external debt was generally low, at 40 per cent of the Gross National Product (GNP). The current account of the balance of payments had narrowed from a deficit of 10 per cent to 5 per cent of GNP, and was expected to improve further. Inflation was at its lowest at 2.1 per cent.

On the financial front, the banking system was sound, as reflected in the strong capitalisation and the high asset quality. The average risk-weighted capital ratio (RWCR) of the banking system was more than 10 per cent, compared to the minimum international standard of 8 per cent. Non-performing loans (NPLs), even using the stringent three-month classification, was only 3.6 per cent of total loans outstanding. The banking system was already subject to strict international prudential standards. Almost all the 25 Core Principles for Effective Banking Supervision recommended by the Bank for International Settlement (BIS) had been adopted. Malaysia's savings rate, at 38 per cent of GDP, was one of the highest in the world. The national savings was sufficient to finance 95 per cent of total investment outlays.

Given the happy environment, the thought of revaluing or devaluing the ringgit never occurred to the government. Malaysia was therefore content to allow the market to determine the exchange rate. With a rock steady economy, political stability and strong business-friendly government, Malaysia believed that the market would not destabilise the ringgit exchange rate.

2. FAIR DISTRIBUTION OF WEALTH

SINCE 1970, Malaysia was actively restructuring its economy in order to give every community a fair share in the wealth of the country. The New Economic Policy (NEP) had been in place since 1970 and had been followed by the National Development Policy (NDP) in 1990. The NDP was intended to further balance the economic well-being of the different communities, this time with emphasis more on quality then quantity.

The privatisation policy had resulted in catapulting a core of *Bumiputeras* or indigenous people into the realm of big business. Many of them were doing well. Over time, we were confident that more *Bumiputeras* would be elevated to this level of business. True, there were some foreigners, a few disgruntled non-*Bumiputera* Malaysians and some Malay socialist politicians who suggested that the NEP only benefited a few friends and family members of the government but few took this allegation seriously.

The Malaysian government is avowedly business-friendly. We think that a business-friendly approach is good for economic development and for increasing the government's revenue. Western commentators, who dismiss the Malaysian policies and practices as crony capitalism, miss the financial rationale for co-operation, for long-term reciprocal relations between firms, banks and the government in a system which intermediates high savings into high corporate debt/equity ratio. A government, which is business-friendly, cannot help but know all the members of the business community. We knew who was good and who was not. When bids were made for contracts or for the privatisation of government entities, the government could not just look at the proposals without looking at the track records of the proposers. In any case, whatever the criteria, in the end only one bidder would win. Labelling anyone who won as a crony of the government placed the government in a no-win situation, since whatever decision that it made would be considered wrong, as the winner, whoever he might be, would, by definition, be branded a crony.

Unlike other countries, Malaysia did not need to sell off government assets to foreigners to raise foreign exchange to pay external debts. Therefore, in Malaysia's privatisation programme, government entities were sold to Malaysians, particularly to *Bumiputeras*, so as to help them make a quick entry into big business. Foreigners were allowed only a minority share in the privatised companies. Given the tremendous potential for profits from privatisation, foreigners were naturally frustrated and unhappy at not getting the lion's share. Their accusation that the Malaysian government was playing favourites was to be expected, and the government's refusal to take notice of this criticism should be understandable.

No one would deny that there had always been some corruption in Malaysia, but the practice was neither widespread nor blatant. Officers and politicians caught for corruption were charged and punished under the relevant provisions of the laws. Corruption in Malaysia had never been such that development or investments were hampered. Foreigners know that they could get their approvals in reasonable time with few hassles. In fact, Malaysia's high rate of growth is the best testimony to the low level of corruption, since in countries where corruption is rife, development, investments and growth would be very slow. Foreign direct investments (FDIs) in Malaysia was one of the highest in the world. In many instances the companies expanded and invested repeatedly. They would have gone elsewhere if the government was corrupt or practised cronyism. They knew very well that had corruption and cronyism been rife, they would have to give free shares in their enterprises to selected personalities. It was not so in Malaysia when many FDIs were wholly foreign-owned, often getting their tax-free licences in less than a week.

The management of Malaysia's finance was applauded by the IMF as late as the second quarter of 1997. Although Malaysia had launched several big infrastructure projects costing billions of ringgit, there was no noticeable increase in foreign borrowings. Malaysia was able to finance most of these projects from domestic sources. The government's external borrowings were low and in many cases Malaysia even prepaid its foreign loans. There was, therefore, no pressure on the government to stop large projects even during the turmoil due to problems in servicing external loans. On the contrary, foreign banks were always anxious to lend more money to the Malaysian government before the turmoil, considering Malaysia as highly creditworthy.

The Malaysian private sector was also free from the burden of large external debts. Given that the Malaysian financial system was flushed with liquidity which meant low interest rates, the major portion of the private sector's financing needs were met through domestic borrowings. The liquidity situation was so strong that even the FDIs were borrowing a significant portion of their capital needs from local sources.

The external reserves were maintained at a high level, capable of financing more than four months of retained imports. This high level of external reserves meant that all of Malaysia's import requirements, whether for capital goods, intermediate goods or consumption goods, could be met without resorting to external borrowings. All in all, at the end of June 1997, the financial situation in Malaysia was very sound. Malaysia was certainly not a candidate for financial or economic turmoil.

When the baht was attacked in June 1997, Malaysia was not unduly worried. We knew that the Malaysian financial situation was much healthier than that of Thailand. In the case of Thailand, the residents had been borrowing large amounts of short-term offshore funds to finance long-term domestic projects in Thailand. This strategy made sense to them since the interest rate of the US dollar was much lower than the baht interest rate. However, this strategy depended entirely on the assumption of a stable baht exchange rate against the US dollar. The attack on the baht forced the Thai central bank to go off the dollar peg and to let the market determine the rate. Immediately the baht was repeatedly devalued.

It was for this reason that the Thai central bank tried to defend the baht during the initial stages of the speculative attack on the currency. The Thai central bank knew that once the peg goes, large companies with heavy external borrowings would suffer substantial currency losses. This is bound to cause a sharp downturn in the economy. The central bank tried very hard to intervene in the foreign exchange market to support the baht, but it failed. The government then decided to float the baht and immediately the baht went into a free fall. When contacted, Malaysia promised to help Thailand overcome its financial crisis with a loan of US$1 billion (RM3.8 billion), of which US$862 million was quickly disbursed. Such was the confidence of Malaysia that it would not be affected by the Thai currency crisis, that it was even willing to provide financial assistance to its neighbour.

3.

SPECULATIVE ATTACK ON THE RINGGIT

A MONTH or so later, i.e. in July 1997, there were ominous talks of contagion. We were told that if the Thai baht fell, then the ringgit would fall too. Why? Well, the fortunes of currencies are infectious, it seems. According to this 'logic', if the baht falls, the production cost in Thailand would be cheaper than in Malaysia. To counter this, Malaysia must devalue the ringgit. And so the currency traders moved in, ahead of the 'expected' devaluation, to shortsell the ringgit which had not been officially pegged to the dollar. The result was rapid trading which induced devaluation. There could have been a little devaluation due to contagion, but it would not have been so rapid and severe. The steep fall in the ringgit exchange rate against the US dollar and other currencies was due to the currency traders' shortselling activities.

A currency has no sensors and cannot possibly know that other currencies are sick. Neither can currencies know that the government is corrupt or practises cronyism. Currencies cannot depreciate themselves. The currency traders depreciate the currencies, not because they fear the currency they hold would depreciate and they would lose their money, but because they see profit in shorting the currencies. Greed, rather than fear, was the motivating factor.

The currency manipulators with large amounts of borrowed funds were not interested in recognising Malaysia's strength. They decided to make a profit on the back of this nebulous concept of 'contagion'. When the crisis hit Thailand, Malaysia's strong economic fundamentals were totally ignored by the market participants. It was the refusal on their part to recognise the important differences that existed amongst regional economies that caused the so-called contagion to spread rapidly. Despite stronger fundamentals, the waves of speculation on the ringgit exchange rate caused it to depreciate sharply against the US dollar. Then the short-term investors in the share market pulled out their capital and caused share prices to fall rapidly, aggravating the economic turmoil through rapid falls in market capitalisation.

When the ringgit began to depreciate against the US dollar, Bank Negara initially intervened to support the ringgit, but quickly stopped intervening as it realised that it was up against forces with very much superior resources. Defending the ringgit could result in a serious depletion of foreign exchange reserves and this would undermine further the value of the ringgit. The free fall, which could follow, would spell economic and financial disaster for the country.

The leadership of the country felt helpless. They correctly identified the currency traders as the culprits behind the depreciation of the ringgit. As can be expected, Malaysian leaders condemned the currency traders for the rogues that they were. The Malaysian leaders were in turn condemned by just about everyone, from the managers of international agencies to self-proclaimed experts and currency traders. All these people maintained, at that time, that the cause of the currency devaluation was bad governance and all that was required to restore confidence and ensure recovery of the currency value and the economy was to replace bad governance with good governance. They completely absolved the currency traders from any responsibility for the problems faced by the former economic tiger. These experts were convinced that the turmoil was temporary. Malaysian leaders were told that they knew nothing about international finance, herd instincts, etc. The Prime Minister was described as a menace to his country.

The currency traders saw themselves as powerful forces in the market and did not take kindly to criticisms of themselves. They claim to be doing a duty to discipline recalcitrant and erring governments. Every time they were criticised by the Malaysians, particularly the Prime Minister, they depressed the value of the ringgit further, along with those of other East Asian currencies. The condemnation of the Malaysian leadership became widespread. At one stage, other East Asian leaders were urged to condemn the Malaysian leader, who had accused the currency traders of currency manipulation. They claim that the Malaysian leader, with his loud mouth, was bringing down not only the value of the ringgit, but also the value of all East Asian currencies.

Leaders of the tiger economies of East Asia, therefore, dissociated themselves from the views of the Malaysian leader. Malaysia was fast becoming a pariah nation to be avoided by everyone.

However, not criticising the currency traders did not spare the other East Asian leaders from having their currencies devalued. It appeared that the future of the East Asian tigers was in the hands of the currency speculators. They were all going to go into an economic and financial free fall which could only be stopped if they handed over the governance of their countries' finance and economy to foreigners, specifically the IMF. There would be no more independent tigers and dragons in East Asia. The 21st century was not going to be the Asian Century.

Many chose to call in the IMF. The loans the IMF gave and the reforms proposed by it were supposed to ensure recovery. Malaysia, however, very early on saw the danger in resorting to the IMF for financial help. We were not willing to surrender the management of our economy to the IMF. We believed the IMF did not understand local conditions and that the problems of different countries were not the same and would not benefit from the same remedy.

More than any other country, Malaysia needed to have control over its economy. Malaysia's economic focus was not only on GDP growth, but also the distributive aspects of growth. We wanted growth with equity, i.e. all the communities in Malaysia must enjoy equitably the economic wealth of the country. Malaysia was involved in a very complex socioeconomic restructuring. In the hands of the IMF, the need for equitable distribution of economic wealth between the races would not receive the attention that was needed. Merely recovering would not be enough for Malaysia. Recovery must be accompanied by the equitable distribution of the economic pie between the *Bumiputeras* and the non-*Bumiputeras*. Failure to do so could result in the kind of race riots which broke out in May 1969. What good would recovery do if the whole country is thrown into perpetual political turmoil and race riots?

There was no way Malaysia would surrender its economy to the IMF, even if that was the only way for the country to achieve economic recovery. Malaysia had to find its own solution to the problems of the devaluation of the ringgit and the shrinkage in market capitalisation which could lead to the destruction of its economy. Hence, Malaysian leaders had to rack their brains to find an alternative solution.

One of the factors which led to Malaysia's rapid growth is its ability to innovate, to plan and to implement its plans effectively. Malaysia had regular five-year plans, long-term 20-year perspective plans and even a 30-year Vision of the future. These were not idle dreams but were clear and practical roadmaps, which were all seriously implemented. It is this ability to plan innovatively and implement the plan on a practical and pragmatic basis that enabled Malaysia with its multiracial population and serious interracial disparities to become stable and to achieve remarkable economic development.

Faced with the traumatic race riots of May 1969, Malaysia set up a National Action Council which devised and implemented the New Economic Policy for growth with equity. To speed up growth, Malaysia conceived the idea of Malaysia Incorporated and very early on discarded state ownership in favour of privatisation.

Now faced with the economic and financial turmoil caused by external forces not within its control, Malaysia came up with the National Economic Recovery Plan (NERP) and set up a National Economic Action Council (NEAC). Opposition leaders were brought into the NEAC. Regular briefings and discussions threw up ideas on how to manage the turmoil.

Meanwhile, the currency continued to be subject to speculative attacks and kept depreciating. Despite shortselling being disallowed by the Kuala Lumpur Stock Exchange (KLSE), the price of Malaysian shares continued to plunge, resulting in margin calls by banks and an increase in non-performing loans. The foreign media gleefully reported the rapid devaluation of the ringgit and the steep plunge in the KLSE Composite Index. It appeared that Malaysia must in the end go to the IMF for help.

The government was getting desperate. It had made a request to Michel Camdessus of the IMF to call for a meeting of finance ministers from developed and developing countries to discuss methods to stabilise the currencies and curb the activities of currency traders. Camdessus told the Malaysian Minister of Finance at that time that he would hold the meeting in April 1998. But nothing happened. No meeting was held.

4.
VIRTUAL IMF POLICY FAILURE

AS the financial crisis continued, it became apparent that the Minister of Finance, aided by the central bank, was implementing policies which were making a bad situation worse. The Minister of Finance and the central bank implemented a number of measures beginning in October 1997 which appeared to reflect the views of the IMF. A credit squeeze was announced by Bank Negara which resulted in banks withdrawing credit and creating a credit crunch. The interest rates were repeatedly increased from single-digit levels to more than 12 per cent per annum. Even companies with viable projects and confirmed export orders found it difficult to obtain financing for operations from the banks. The central bank shortened the default period for the classification of non-performing loans from six months to three months, creating further problems for banks and businesses. The prudential requirements of banks were further tightened by requiring them to increase the general provision for bad and doubtful debts from 1 per cent to 1.5 per cent of total loans.

The Minister of Finance and the central bank further restricted consumer spending by imposing a maximum margin of 70 per cent for financing the purchase of passenger vehicles. In addition, the maximum repayment period for hire-purchase loans for vehicles was restricted to five years.

Construction activities, which were very important for GDP growth, were also restricted by the Minister of Finance and the central bank. The banks were not allowed to grant loans for any property project, where construction had not yet started. Even in the case of property projects where construction had started, the banks were urged by the central bank to review the viability and reduce the amount of financing.

The central bank, in continuing to maintain a high statutory reserves ratio (SRR) in the face of a tightening liquidity situation, was pushing even profitable banks into a loss-making situation. RM52 billion worth of SRR was kept in the central bank earning nothing. If it lent to the banks it charged a rate of 12 per cent per annum, creating unnecessary losses for the banks.

The government requested the central bank to ease the liquidity situation by reducing the SRR from 13.5 per cent to 10 per cent. The central bank complied, but immediately sabotaged the objective by withdrawing an equivalent amount from the interbank market so that on a net basis there was no additional liquidity in the system. The central bank even went further, a few days later, by instructing the banks that whatever extra funds they had, following the reduction of the SRR from 13.5 per cent to 10 per cent, had to be used to reduce their interbank borrowings rather than lending to their clients. Therefore, the reduction in the SRR, which was intended to have a positive affect on the liquidity of the banks, was manipulated by the central bank to worsen further the credit crunch situation in the country.

It was pointed out to the Minister of Finance that his Ministry and the central bank were causing the economy to shrink and the government may not get sufficient revenue to run the administration. But he was certain that his "virtual IMF" policy would save the economy.

By April 1998, the economic crisis in the country had worsened, with the ringgit continuing to depreciate towards 4.80 against the US dollar. The stock market was continuing its downward slide and the credit crunch situation was becoming unbearable due to the central bank's tightening measures. The Prime Minister's view, at that time, was that action should be taken by the Minister of Finance and the central bank to provide relief to the banks and their clients through measures that would ease the situation. However, instead of providing relief, the central bank, on April 27, 1998, announced the following measures to tighten the situation even further:

1. The minimum risk-weighted capital ratio of finance companies (who were the worst affected by the crisis) was raised from 8.5 per cent to 9.00 per cent.
2. The minimum capital funds of the finance companies was raised from RM5 million to RM300 million to be complied with by the end of June 1999 and subsequently to RM600 million by the end of 2000.
3. The single-customer limit of the financial institutions was reduced from 30 per cent to 25 per cent of the financial institutions' capital funds.

On the fiscal side, the Minister of Finance reduced government expenditure by 21 per cent, which virtually stopped development work altogether, as salaries, which made up 80 per cent of the government's budget, could not be cut. No developmental expenditure meant no contracts for many construction companies and their suppliers. This, together with the other measures of the central bank, meant bankruptcy for many companies.

The sum effect of all the measures above was that the banks and businesses which were already suffering from the currency crisis were pushed into a situation of dire distress. What the Minister of Finance, together with the central bank, had done was to implement a virtual IMF without the IMF loans; namely, a combination of tight monetary and fiscal policies, raising the interest rate to defend the exchange rate, attempting to strengthen the banking system through more stringent prudential standards and cutting down public expenditure to improve the current-account balance. As a result of the implementations of these standard IMF prescriptions, Malaysia's economy plunged deeper into recession. Business was almost at a standstill and the government revised downwards the expected revenue from corporate taxes for the following year. The foreign media praised the Minister of Finance for implementing a virtual IMF policy. Everyone was gleefully predicting that the time was near for Malaysia to go to the IMF for help and to surrender economic control to the IMF. Malaysia, it was felt, had no choice but to open up its economy to foreigners without conditions. There would be rich pickings for foreign capitalists, including those who had invested in the hedge funds.

The 'recalcitrance' of the Malaysian leader was also now coming under criticism by a segment of the local population, who wanted the leader to bow out and give the reins to his deputy, who was also the Finance Minister. Supporters of the Deputy Prime Minister accused the government and by implication the Prime Minister of cronyism, nepotism and corruption. The message for the Prime Minister was clear. The economy would not recover unless he stepped down and handed the reins of government to his Deputy. However, the Prime Minister did not seem to get the message.

The government was desperate, but it was not about to capitulate. It undertook certain measures to prevent further deterioration of the economy. All salary increases were stopped; travel abroad for Ministers and other government staff was curtailed and allowances were reduced. There was even an attempt to reduce sugar consumption and the import of food and other products. All these measures were not at all effective. They merely lowered the consumption level and the standard of living of the people. The importers, dealers and retailers all suffered. In the end, the government too would feel the crunch through reduced revenue.

Construction, retail sales, purchases of property and motor vehicles went down very badly. Fortunately, Malaysian workers were not laid off in a big way, as demand for Malaysian-manufactured goods, mainly electronics, remained high. For many years Malaysia had become short of workers and was forced to allow almost two million foreign workers into the country. Although a number of Malaysians lost their jobs, the brunt of the slowdown was felt by the foreign workers, many of whom could not find employment and had to return to their countries.

The fact that the economies of the developed countries were not affected and were actually doing better during this time helped the Malaysian economy by enabling Malaysia to increase its exports. Exports of palm oil (sold in US dollars) earned more ringgit because of the weaker exchange rate as well as higher demand. In ringgit terms, and even in foreign currency terms, Malaysia very quickly achieved a current-account surplus, something that it could not achieve before because of the large deficit in the services account.

The Prime Minister came up with a wild idea to resolve the crisis. To counter the devaluation, he toyed with the idea of raising income by increasing salaries and wages and allowing prices of goods and services to be increased proportionately. He was aware that this would lead to an inflationary spiral, but he felt that the government would be able to manage the inflation so as to be less than the devaluation of the ringgit. The downside of such a move was that the cost of production in Malaysia would increase and affect exports, as well as profit from exports. The concept was shot down by other members of the government on the grounds that it was not practical and was likely to lead to galloping inflation.

The NEAC had set up an Executive Committee consisting of the Prime Minister, Deputy Prime Minister cum Finance Minister, the Minister with Special Functions, the Deputy Governor of Bank Negara Malaysia (for some reason the Governor never attended), the Director-General of the Economic Planning Unit (EPU), the head of a Malaysian think-tank and a person from the business sector. Subsequently, the Adviser to the central bank and the Second Minister of Finance were also appointed to the Committee. The Committee was charged with overseeing the economic and financial performance of the country, and to decide and act when necessary. The Committee met every morning during the crisis to review all relevant financial, economic and trade figures. Briefings were made by government agencies. The Committee was empowered to act quickly, where necessary, without waiting for Cabinet approval.

5.
UNDERSTANDING CURRENCY TRADING

ONE of the measures decided upon by the Committee was to revive trade with the Asean neighbours. All the Asean countries were in financial trouble and did not have enough foreign exchange to finance imports. The mechanism of bilateral payments arrangement was to be utilised, in which the gross two-way trade flows are netted off every three months and the net balance settled in the exporters' currency. The payment was to be made between the two respective central banks. The exporter would be paid in local currency by his central bank immediately on export and the importer will pay his central bank also in his local currency. The mechanism of bilateral payments arrangement had already been in place for many years between Malaysia and many developing countries. The arrangement was pioneered by Malaysia and had helped to increase Malaysia's trade with its non-traditional trading partners by up to 400 per cent. The only difference between the existing practice and the proposed arrangement for Asean countries was that, while previously settlement of the net balance was in US dollars, now the Asean countries which were in turmoil and short of foreign exchange, would settle their payments in local currencies.

The Prime Minister travelled to Bangkok, Manila and Jakarta to put this proposal to the Prime Minister and the Presidents of the countries concerned. The proposal was accepted, subject to the laws and practices of the countries concerned. Unfortunately, the bureaucratic process took too long and the proposed bilateral payments arrangement was not implemented.

In the meantime, the economy continued to deteriorate and the ringgit kept getting further devalued along with the currencies of Indonesia, Thailand, the Philippines and South Korea. It seemed at times that this devaluation would go on and on and Malaysia would sink deeper into economic recession. There appeared to be no limit to the power of the hedge funds to destroy any economy in order to make the much touted 30 per cent return for their investors.

6.

UNDERSTANDING THE COMPLEX FOREX MARKET

MALAYSIA continued to believe that the root cause of the economic and financial turmoil was the currency trading by the hedge funds and banks. If something was to be done by the country on its own to counter the hedge funds, the mechanism of currency trading had to be fully understood, and a plan devised to beat the currency speculators at their own game. Unfortunately, the person in the central bank (with the rank of Adviser) who had international experience in foreign exchange trading had left the central bank in 1994.

Perhaps, at this stage, the story of the foray of Bank Negara into the foreign exchange market between 1985 and 1993 needs to be told. Up to 1985, Bank Negara did not actively manage its external reserves. However, this situation changed after the Plaza Accord of 1985 when the G7 countries decided to strengthen the Japanese yen in order to make Japan less competitive. Malaysia, which had significant borrowings denominated in yen, suffered heavy losses. In order to offset losses arising from the decisions of the G7 countries, Bank Negara started to manage its external reserves actively, including taking foreign exchange positions. Bank Negara's senior adviser was put in charge. The foreign exchange activities were limited to the currencies of the G7 countries. It did not deal in the currencies of the developing countries. Given the large liquidity available in the currencies of the G7 countries, Bank Negara's transactions did not have any material effect on the exchange rates of the G7 currencies. Bank Negara did very well in its foreign exchange trading activities and made large profits. It became very well known in the international foreign exchange market as a savvy foreign exchange trader. Its trading activity was, however, condemned by some financial experts who later supported the currency trading activities which damaged the economies of the Asian tigers. Clearly, it is not what is done which is wrong but who is doing it.

Unfortunately, during the international currency turmoil following the non-ratification of the Maastricht Treaty by Denmark in 1992, Bank Negara suffered losses. The Adviser resigned from Bank Negara Malaysia. The government instructed Bank Negara to discontinue foreign exchange trading. It is indeed a strange twist of history that this costly experience in the foreign exchange market provided Malaysia with the knowledge and skill required to implement the selective exchange control regime in order to frustrate the currency traders and help the country's economic recovery.

The former Adviser of the central bank was summoned by the Prime Minister for a briefing. Following a series of meetings between the Prime Minister and the Adviser, the Prime Minister understood, for the first time since the crisis, the complex and complicated workings of the foreign exchange market, including the way the prices were quoted, the psychological factors that motivate the currency traders (greed and fear) and the concept of offshore currency. The Prime Minister's understanding of the foreign exchange market was essential in devising a plan to save Malaysia from currency speculators and the IMF.

It now became obvious that some of the information that was presented by the Minister of Finance to the government, including figures on large outflows of ringgit in the form of cash to Singapore, was misleading. The Minister of Finance did not fully understand the concept of offshore ringgit. He thought that the term 'offshore ringgit' referred to the physical ringgit overseas, mainly in Singapore. The central bank either did not enlighten him or it too did not understand. In any case, the central bank did not stop the Minister and the government from instructing Customs officials to search travellers crossing the border for cash on their persons. This silly action did not stop the ringgit from going abroad and being traded.

The difference between offshore ringgit and domestic ringgit is not whether the ringgit is physically in Malaysia or outside Malaysia. Except for small amounts of cash held by moneychangers and banks, the ringgit will always be in Malaysia physically. When the ringgit is sold by a non-resident to another non-resident, all that happens is a change in ownership from the seller to the buyer in the accounts of the Malaysian bank and the foreign bank. No cash changed hands, only book entries in the banks of the buyer and seller changed.

When the currency trader borrows the ringgit, the same thing happens. The lender, usually a foreign international bank, merely transfers the ownership of the ringgit to the borrower in the books of the bank and the Malaysian bank holding the ringgit. The trader can then short the ringgit, delivering only after the ringgit has devalued, again through transfer to the accounts of the buyer.

Being able to leverage by 20 times their capital explains the strength of the hedge funds, i.e. they use a geared position to fight the central banks which use only their cash position. The hedge funds also tend to act together, buying and selling to each other and appreciating or depreciating the ringgit as they wish in order to maximise their profits. They do not buy the ringgit or any other currency in order to pay for goods or services. They really have no use for the money except to speculate and manipulate it. For them, money is a commodity like any other commodity traded on commodity exchanges. As in commodity futures, the physical existence of the currency is not important.

It became a matter of urgency for Malaysia to do something drastic to protect itself from the currency speculators. Borrowing from the IMF was not an option. The money would largely be used to repay debts to foreign banks. It was just transferring the debt to the IMF and Malaysia would still have to find money to pay off the IMF later. 'Graduating' from this would take decades, and during that time the country would have to take orders from the IMF, losing its financial independence.

The first serious attempt made by Malaysia to combat the greedy currency speculators, who were having a one-way bet, was to make them aware that selling the ringgit need not be a one-way bet all the time. There was a need to identify some sources of supply of US dollars which could be sold for ringgits to offset the purchase of US dollars against ringgits by the currency speculators. A decision had already been made that the central bank should not use its external reserves to intervene. Fortunately, Malaysia has a number of companies with large export proceeds and these companies are natural sellers of US dollars. All that was required was to coordinate their sales of US dollars in such a way as to catch the shortsellers offguard, and trigger the element of fear in them, so that they would buy back the ringgit that they had shortsold, fearing that it would appreciate and cause them to lose money. Of course, when they buy the ringgit it would appreciate further.

When this strategy was put into effect, it worked initially. The slide of the ringgit stopped and subsequently the ringgit began to appreciate towards the rate of 3.00 against the US dollar. It looked as if the ringgit could go back to its original level of 2.50. At this point, the hedge funds, realising what was afoot, came back with a vengeance. They sold larger and larger amounts of the ringgit. Malaysian companies could not sustain their defence of the ringgit against the multibillion-dollar hedge funds and the large foreign banks which allowed them to leverage up to 20 times their capital. Considering that the Quantum Fund and the Long-Term Credit Management (LTCM) Fund were capitalised at around US$10 billion (RM38 billion), leveraging by 20 times really means that they have virtually unlimited capital resources to counter any attempt by locals to roll back the devaluation. Very quickly the companies gave up the attempt to defend the ringgit.

Since the first strategy did not work, something else had to be tried. The government considered a proposal to peg the ringgit against the yen, but pegging was not possible as long as the ringgit was freely available to the currency traders to manipulate.

Finally, it was decided that the only remaining option was to impose selective exchange control. Early in 1998, a proposal was made for a broad framework of exchange-control measures.

The most crucial element in ensuring that currency control would work was to prevent the ringgit from getting into the hands of currency traders.

The ringgit, as had been explained, never leaves the country. This is because the ringgit is not valid tender in other countries. The physical ringgit outside the country is only useful for exchanging with other currencies by people who want to take it back into Malaysia where it can be used to purchase things. Moneychangers and foreign banks may keep small amounts of cash for changing with travellers wishing to visit Malaysia.

Larger amounts to be taken into Malaysia may be by a bank order which can be drawn on a Malaysian bank. The foreign bank would receive from the buyer the equivalent amount in foreign currency before issuing a bank order to transfer the ringgit to the buyer's account in the Malaysian bank.

The manner with which the currency traders buy and sell ringgit have already been explained. Such transactions are anything but transparent. They are also very fast now as they are done on the banks' computers. Literally hundreds of millions of dollars can change hands within a few seconds across numerous borders.

If we have to prevent the currency traders from getting their hands on the ringgit, we can only do so through the Malaysian banks which are subject to directives by the Malaysian central bank. After studying the *modus operandi* of the currency traders, it was decided that since any ringgit transaction abroad must be reflected in the books of Malaysian banks where the physical ringgit is held, these Malaysian banks and foreign banks operating in Malaysia should be instructed not to transfer the ringgit from one account to another. The legal ownership of the ringgit would remain with the owner of the ringgit at the time the controls were imposed, regardless of his sale of his ringgit. The buyer will not be entitled to the ringgit he has bought. Effectively this meant no offshore transaction in ringgit was possible.

The sales of ringgit outside Malaysia stopped abruptly. There were some last-minute purchases of the ringgit by the currency traders in expectation of the government revaluing the currency. As a result, the ringgit appreciated slightly. The other Asian currencies also appreciated as there was general fear that other countries would follow Malaysia's example. But of course these countries were under IMF control and could not take independent action.

When the ringgit was traded at 3.80 to the US dollar, the government announced that that would be the rate of exchange between the ringgit and the US dollar.

But all was not smooth sailing in developing this strategy to fix the ringgit exchange rate by depriving the currency traders of access to the currency. The proposal was debated at length in the NEAC Committee. Initially most of the members were against it. The Deputy Governor of the central bank contended that the International Financial Institutions (IFIs) and even the rich countries would retaliate in some way.

Malaysia would be a pariah, shunned by the world's banks. It would not be able to borrow should it need money for whatever reason. Interest rates on such loans would be raised to prohibitive levels. It was hinted that sanctions might be applied against Malaysia.

Additionally, Malaysia had to pay for imports. Would there be sufficient foreign exchange to pay for these? Dependent as it is for capital and intermediate goods in order to manufacture for exports, inability to pay for imports would reduce Malaysia's exports and inflow of foreign exchange.

What if all the investors, both short and long term, were to pull out. Malaysia's economy would collapse. There was the possibility of legal action being taken against Malaysia by a host of people adversely affected by the controls. Malaysia would not be able to defend itself.

One member of the Committee came up with 32 reasons why Malaysia should not attempt to control the exchange rate in the way that was proposed. Although all the arguments were demolished the fear was real and the possible problems which the country would be faced with were frightening.

At that time the political situation in Malaysia was still stable. The Deputy Prime Minister and Finance Minister was still with the government. Nevertheless, if the proposed controls failed, then the government's credibility would be shattered and the government party might lose in the next election.

Throughout the discussions, the Deputy Governor of the central bank was unconvinced and opposed the controls. When it was pointed out that China has such restriction on trading of its currency he argued that whereas China had never freed its currency, the ringgit had been floated a long time and controlling it would be a step backward.

Eventually, with various degree of reluctance, it was decided that the controls should be imposed. The central bank was naturally given the task of implementing the various measures, the principal of which was to instruct banks in Malaysia not to transfer ringgit to any account when instructed to do so by their client's banks abroad. Bank Negara was to supervise the management of ringgit owned by foreigners very strictly to prevent any leakage. The ringgits owned by foreigners could, however, be used to buy anything within the country and to export the goods purchased. This simply meant releasing the ringgit into the market and increasing liquidity. In this way, much of the money which was being used to speculate would be returned to Malaysia, enabling Malaysian banks to lend to locals.

The ringgit could not be taken out of the country in any form. However, dividends or proceeds from the sale of assets in the country was allowed to be taken out in foreign currency at 3.80 to a US dollar to be obtained from the banking system or central bank. The sale of assets during such times would not be easy as there were few local buyers and the prices would not be good. Sales to foreigners would involve inflow of funds and would not affect the reserves when the foreign exchange is taken out.

7.
THE CLOB FACTOR

IT has been mentioned that the economic turmoil was also the result of short-term investors pulling out their investments in the KLSE. Shares had plummeted, resulting in a very serious reduction in market capitalisation. At the time the currency turmoil began, the market was worth more than RM800 billion or about US$320 billion, at 2.50 ringgit per US dollar. As soon as the ringgit was subjected to attacks and was devalued, share prices on the KLSE started to fall. The Composite Index was at about 1,000 points in early 1997. By the end of 1997 it had dipped to around 600.

The government tried to stop the slide by making short-selling illegal. But still the share prices went down. It was apparent that there was a leakage and that leakage could only be due to shares being sold on the Singapore over-the-counter market called CLOB (Central Limit Order Book), set up by the Singapore authorities to market Malaysian shares when the Stock Exchange of Singapore (SES) was separated from the KLSE in 1989.

Sales of shares on the KLSE have to be registered with the Central Depository System (CDS) accounts in Malaysia. Such sales are subjected to conditions imposed by Malaysian authorities. Malaysian brokers and the KLSE benefit from commissions charged. Sales in Singapore would not of course benefit Malaysians or the government.

Although the Malaysian government objected to the setting up and the operation of CLOB, no serious attempt was made to stop the activities of this over-the-counter trading in Malaysian shares in Singapore. Even when frequent rumours were started in Singapore which caused share prices to dip and then to recover when the rumours were found to be unfounded, the Malaysian authorities did nothing. Obviously, speculators in Singapore were making a lot of money from these rumours and the subsequent fluctuation of the share prices.

But when the currency turmoil started, the drop in share prices became more acute despite the ban on shortselling. Suspecting CLOB for the failure of the ban, the former central bank Adviser was requested to study in detail the mechanism through which Malaysian shares were traded on CLOB. It was discovered that CLOB was owned by the Central Depository (Pte) Ltd in Singapore (CDPL). All shares purchased through CLOB goes into the CDPL, which had CDS accounts with Malaysian brokers, but the bulk of the custody was with Hwang-DBS Bhd in Penang. The beneficial owners of CLOB shares in Singapore did not have legal ownership of the shares as far as the Malaysian CDS is concerned. What they had was a statement from the CDPL, which confirmed to them on a monthly basis their stockholdings, including Malaysian shares purchased at CLOB.

Since the trustees of the share owners remained the same, transactions on CLOB would not be reflected on the CDS. The CDPL of Singapore could also lend the shares for shortselling in CLOB and the Malaysian CDS would not be any wiser. Yet the prices on CLOB affects the KLSE share prices.

In order to stop CLOB, registration of ownership through trustees was disallowed. Owners of shares must all register in their own name. Shares acquired through CLOB were not allowed to be traded until the owners register with the CDS. This meant that registration in the name of trustees could not be made and the buyer of shares would not be entitled to the shares bought until they were registered in the owners' name with the CDS. Effectively this stopped the operations of CLOB.

Having decided what to do to stop the trading in Malaysian currency and the activities of CLOB, there remained the need to implement these measures. Naturally the central bank had to be the principal implementing authority. A last-minute bid was made by the Governor of the central bank and his deputy to stop the control measures. Both of them resigned. The government had to quickly authorise the Assistant Governor to act as head of the central bank and to implement the measures.

8. HOW SELECTIVE EXCHANGE CONTROLS WORK

ON September 2, 1998, the controls came into effect. The world was shocked and practically everyone, including, of course, the great economic and financial experts predicted the total collapse of the Malaysian economy. It was madness for Malaysia, a small developing country, to go against the rest of the world, almost.

What exactly were the selective exchange control measures? Actually the measures were minimal. There were only three measures, namely:

1. The offshore ringgit market was eliminated and currency speculators no longer had access to ringgit funds. This was done by 'freezing' the external ringgit accounts of the non-residents in Malaysia. They were not allowed to sell or lend the ringgit to another non-resident but could invest their funds freely in Malaysia. Thus the currency traders were unable to shortsell the ringgit and change its exchange rate. Only the government could determine the exchange rate.

2. The government fixed the exchange rate at RM3.80 to the US dollar.
3. A "twelve-month rule" was imposed prohibiting the repatriation of portfolio funds for twelve months. This "twelve-month rule" was necessary given the prevailing instability of the financial market. There was the possibility that the bad publicity following Malaysia's "unorthodox" measures could result in massive short-term capital outflows. A twelve-month restriction was therefore considered necessary. However, when the situation stabilised six months down the road, this "twelve-month rule" was replaced (for new funds) with a levy and subsequently even this levy was diluted further to apply only to dividends repatriated. Interestingly, when the twelve-month rule expired in September 1999 there was no massive outflow. The market perception had obviously changed dramatically between September 1998 and September 1999. Foreign investors were happy with the appreciation of their shares in the KLSE and the general performance of the Malaysian economy.

The primary objective of Malaysia's selective exchange control regime implemented in September 1998 was for Malaysia to regain control of its economy from the currency speculators and manipulators, so that Malaysians can decide the destiny of Malaysia. The measures implemented were very carefully crafted so as to optimise the positive aspects of globalisation and remove the negative aspects of globalisation. The positive aspects of globalisation that were retained were the complete freedom in matters of international trade and FDIs. The liberal regime that governed trade transactions and FDIs were left unchanged. The negative aspects of globalisation that were eliminated were the offshore market for the trading of ringgit and the free flow of short-term funds that destabilises the economy.

The government fixed the ringgit exchange rate at 3.80 to the US dollar, the rate which prevailed at the time the controls were imposed.

The government could have fixed the ringgit at the old rate of 2.50 against the US dollar. This would have enriched Malaysia and Malaysians. However, such a strong level for the ringgit would have made Malaysia less competitive relative to its neighbours. The ringgit's exchange rate of 3.80 against the US dollar restored the previous rate of 1:10 against the baht and the peso. True, imported goods priced in US dollars would be more expensive at RM3.80 compared to RM2.50, but this is actually good for the Malaysian economy. While imports would be reduced, exports would increase, and, therefore, a trade surplus would be easier to achieve. Indeed, Malaysia's trade surplus has never been bigger than now.

Once CLOB was put out of action by the new rules in September 1998, the prices on the KLSE rallied strongly. The KLSE CI rose quickly from 262 to above 800 and market capitalisation increased substantially. Malaysian investors of listed companies saw the value of their shares appreciate significantly, and the margin calls became a thing of the past. Those who needed to raise cash had no problem in selling their shares at very much higher prices then before.

The holders of shares bought through CLOB were not able to sell their shares immediately after the closure of CLOB in September 1998 as logistical arrangements had to be worked out to migrate the shares to the CDS in Kuala Lumpur on an individual basis. The migration was completed in the middle of the year 2000. During the period, the value of shares had increased by more than 300 per cent. The holders of CLOB shares should really be grateful to the government of Malaysia for delaying the sale of their shares.

The same is true with the "twelve-month rule" imposed on the non-resident investors in the KLSE, which prohibited them from repatriating their capital for twelve months. If the "twelve-month rule" was not imposed, the non-residents would have sold their shares at very much lower prices and repatriated their funds. As a result of the "twelve-month rule", most foreign investors could not sell their shares and today, they are able to enjoy the greatly appreciated prices of the shares they hold. Given that their holdings accounted for 30 per cent of the KLSE's capitalisation, had they sold their shares in 1998, this would have resulted in a sharp downturn in the KLSE and a depletion of Malaysia's external reserves. This would have destabilised the Malaysian economy and would have made the subsequent recovery that much more difficult. The "twelve-month rule" therefore created a win-win situation for both the non-resident investors and the Malaysian government.

An important point that needs emphasising is that FDIs were not subject to the selective exchange control measures in any way. They were allowed not only to repatriate their profits but were also allowed to repatriate the proceeds from the sale of their assets, if they chose to do so. It must be noted that the rules for FDIs in Malaysia do not require the FDIs to bring in 100 per cent of the capital to meet all their financing needs. For every ringgit they bring in, they are allowed to borrow RM3 from the banks in Malaysia. The selective exchange control measures did not change this policy. Malaysia is able to be liberal in this respect because it has large external reserves, as well as ample liquidity in the domestic financial system. The most important consideration in Malaysia's policy towards the FDIs is job creation and technology transfer. The foreign exchange inflow aspect of the FDIs was never an important consideration in Malaysia's policy towards FDIs. In order to ensure that the local borrowing of the FDIs is not entirely with the subsidiaries of foreign banks operating in Malaysia, a 60:40 rule was imposed which requires the

FDIs to meet at least 60 per cent of their domestic borrowings from Malaysian-owned banks in Malaysia.

This liberal policy of allowing the FDIs to borrow from banks in Malaysia has also brought about a win-win situation. They are good paymasters, and banks in Malaysia, including Malaysian-owned banks, make good profit by lending to them. Given that Malaysia has a high savings rate of 38 per cent of GDP, the banks have a need to lend a significant portion of the national savings.

However, an interesting phenomenon of FDIs in Malaysia is that they invariably add on to their investments in Malaysia either through new capital or through the retention and ploughing back of their profits. Even during the bad patch of the 1997-1998 financial crisis, the FDIs in Malaysia continued to increase their investments.

Malaysia's policy on the repatriation of export proceeds need to be explained, as this was an important factor in Malaysia's ability to implement the selective exchange control regime in September 1998. Government regulation requires exporters (including FDIs) to repatriate their export proceeds back to Malaysia immediately when the export proceeds are received. There are some exceptions given to this repatriation requirement, but these exceptions are very minor. Exporters are allowed to give credit to their importers for a maximum of 6 months. This means that, within 6 months after the date of export, at the latest, all export proceeds are repatriated back to Malaysia and sold to banks in Malaysia. The banks in Malaysia, after meeting the demands from the importers, will sell the net balance to the central bank daily. This policy has resulted in a convincing build-up of Malaysia's external reserves over the years, and gave Malaysia the confidence to implement the selective exchange control regime in September 1998 on the basis of a strong external reserves position. It should be noted that the combination of a liberal attitude of allowing the FDIs to borrow from the domestic financial system and strictly forbidding them to retain their export proceeds overseas has resulted in Malaysian banks being able to recycle the high level of Malaysian savings and the central bank to build up its external reserves.

Having stabilised the currency market through the selective exchange control measures and having stabilised the KLSE through the closure of CLOB, the government had the opportunity, from September 1998 onwards, to focus more directly on reviving the economy.

9. REVIVING THE ECONOMY

THE non-performing loans (NPLS) of the banking system by that time had risen from 4.7 per cent at the end of 1997 to 13.2 per cent. The capital strength of banking institutions had been severely tested with eleven of them requiring new capital injection. The performance of the banking system was badly affected with 46 banking institutions registering losses. The total loss registered by the banking system amounted to RM2.3 billion.

The following chronology of events reflect the fast gear that was engaged by the Executive Committee of the NEAC to revive the economy:

- *September 1, 1998*
  The statutory reserves requirement was reduced from 8 per cent to 6 per cent, injecting RM8 billion into the financial system.
- *September 3, 1998*
  The BNM intervention rate was reduced from 9.5 per cent to 8 per cent per annum to bring about an equivalent lowering of interest rates across the board in the financial system. The liquid asset ratio requirement

was also reduced from 17 per cent to 15 per cent, freeing RM8 billion of liquid assets that could be sold by the financial institutions to fund their operations. The requirement for commercial banks to maintain their *vostro* balances with the central bank was uplifted and this provided extra liquidity to the banks of more than RM1 billion.

- *September 8, 1998*
  Loans for the purchase and construction of houses costing RM250,000 and below were exempted from the 20 per cent limit on lending to the broad property sector to further stimulate the construction sector.
- *September 15, 1998*
  The maximum margin over the quoted Base Lending Rate (BLR) was reduced from 4 percentage points to 2.5 percentage points to lower the lending rate for companies and individuals so as to facilitate viable projects and encourage consumption as well as reduce the interest servicing burden of companies.
- *September 16, 1998*
  The SRR was reduced from 6 per cent to 4 per cent, releasing another RM8 billion into the economy.
- *September 23, 1998*
  The limit for financial institutions on lending for the purchase of shares and unit trust funds was increased from 15 per cent to 20 per cent of total outstanding loans so as to encourage investment in the KLSE.
- *September 25, 1998*
  The non-performing loan classification was lengthened from 3 months to 6 months to provide borrowers with some breathing space to regularise their accounts.
- *October 5, 1998*
  The BNM intervention rate was reduced from 8 per cent to 7.5 per cent per annum, to lower further the general interest rate level in the system. The maximum

margin of financing of 60 per cent imposed on loans for the purchase of residential properties and land was abolished, so as to give a boost to the property sector which had a serious overhang as a result of the crisis.

- *October 13, 1998*
  The Loan Complaints and Monitoring Unit (LCMU) was established in Bank Negara Malaysia to assist borrowers facing difficulties in securing financing.
- *November 10, 1998*
  The BNM intervention rate was reduced from 7.5 per cent to 7 per cent per annum to reduce further the interest rate level in the financial system.
- *November 19, 1998*
  The government established a RM750 million "Rehabilitation Fund for Small and Medium Industries", to provide financial assistance to viable small and medium industries (SMIs) which were facing temporary cashflow problems.
- *November 20, 1998*
  The minimum monthly repayment of credit cards was reduced from 10 per cent to 5 per cent to promote consumer spending.
- *November 21, 1998*
  Every banking institution was required to set up a "Special Loans Rehabilitation Unit" to assist borrowers who had problems repaying their loans. The maximum margin of financing of 85 per cent for passenger cars costing RM40,000 and below was abolished.
- *December 5, 1998*
  BNM reduced the maximum lending rate under the Small and Medium Industries Fund and the Special Scheme for Low and Medium Cost Houses from 10 per cent to 8.5 per cent.

The Executive Committee of the NEAC gave particular attention to the operations of Danaharta (Assets Management Company), Danamodal (Bank Refinancing Company) and the Corporate Debt Restructuring Committee (CDRC) which had all been set up during the crisis, to address the problems of non-performing loans and bank recapitalisation. The role of Danaharta was to carve out the NPLs from the banking system so that the banks could refocus on their function of lending to revive the economy. The role of Danamodal was to recaptilise the financial institutions and thereby restore the capital strength of the banking system to a much healthier level. The role of CDRC was to provide a platform for companies and banks to come together and work out a debt restructuring programme in an informal manner.

Once the selective exchange control measures were implemented, the three organisations went into high gear. By March 31, 1999, Danaharta had acquired NPLs amounting to RM16 billion, Danamodal had recapitalised ten banking institutions amounting to RM6.2 billion, and the CDRC was fully focused on the restructuring of a number of large companies.

The Executive Committee of the NEAC scrutinised every aspect of the economy daily. Figures on trade performance, external reserves, interest rates, lending by banks, sales of property and motor vehicles, retail sales, tonnage and containers handled by the ports, passengers and freight at the airports, details of goods manufactured and exported, details on imports, new businesses registered and bankruptcies, unemployment and job vacancies, wages, government projects and contracts, electricity consumed, etc, were all laid out daily before the Committee for discussion. Quite often specific actions were immediately taken. When motor vehicles were not selling well the Committee decided on special hire-purchase terms and ensured that the prices were right.

Two property ownership campaigns were held to reduce the large overhang in the property sector. The first campaign was held in December 1998 and the second in October 1999. The developers participated enthusiastically in the property fairs, bringing in their models and brochures and equipping their booths with many sales people. Banks, insurance companies, lawyers and government officers concerned with registration of property sales and other legal procedures were all brought under one roof. A total value of RM6.4 billion of properties were sold during the two campaigns. This result was gratifying for everyone, including the government, which knows very well the adverse side effect of a big property overhang.

When retail sales were low, the government gave a temporary allowance of RM600 to all its employees. The allowance was disbursed at RM100 per month to ensure that it is spent in the country for the purchase of daily necessities. The local retailers benefited from this extra purchasing power of government employees.

Complaints of the business community were heard by the Executive Committee and frequent briefings were given by various government agencies and by the private sector. Very often immediate actions were taken, always with the objective of ensuring that nothing stood in the way of a quick turnaround towards a path of rapid growth.

It is now two years since Malaysia imposed selective capital controls and the signs are clear that the controls have successfully stopped the currency traders and the short-term investors from doing any more damage to the Malaysian economy. The exchange rate of the ringgit has remained fixed at 3.80 to the US dollar and the composite index of the KLSE has risen from 262 points in September 1998 to around 800 now. The companies and the banks have nearly all recovered. Confidence has returned and people have money to spend once again.

All the economic activities have revived, and the construction cranes are moving again. Motor vehicle sales have returned to pre-turmoil levels. Indeed all signs indicate a robust economic recovery.

In 1997, when the recession began, growth of the GDP was still high at 7.5 per cent as the downturn affected only the second half of the year. 1998 was the most serious year when the GDP shrank by 7.2 per cent. But 1999 showed distinct recovery with the GDP returning to 5.6 per cent. It is expected that this year the GDP will achieve at least 5.8 per cent as projected by the government.

10.
STRONG RECOVERY AND LESSONS LEARNT

MALAYSIA has recovered and recovered very fast and very strongly. The experts who had predicted disaster for Malaysia when it imposed selective capital controls are now either silent or have grudgingly admitted that the controls work and enabled Malaysia to recover strongly.

Lately the IMF has commended Malaysia for solving its economic problem through the selective capital controls devised by itself. Even George Soros who had condemned Malaysia and its leadership for singling out the currency traders as the culprits responsible for devaluing currencies and damaging the economies of countries, now admit that Malaysia had done the right thing in not submitting to the IMF and the standard formula that it prescribed for all economic ailments.

Strangely enough, Soros, the archetypal rogue currency trader, has actually agreed that currency trading needs to be regulated and that the market is imperfect and cannot be relied on to determine exchange rates. But the IMF and the economically and financially powerful countries of the West are still adamant that the freedom to trade in currencies must be maintained.

Freedom is sacred and must in no way be curbed. It is an article of faith that must never be questioned.

There can be no doubt that currency trading had caused terrible damage to the economies of the countries whose currencies were devalued by the traders. In several instances, the financial and economic turmoil due to devaluation was accompanied by massive unemployment, shortages of food and fuel, demonstrations, riots, the burning of business premises, looting, rape and murder. Governments were overthrown to be replaced by shaky governments which not only submitted to the IMF and Western control, but were unable to restore law and order or to bring about a turnaround of the economy. And these are countries whose governments previously demonstrated their ability to develop their countries until they became known as economic tigers. Still the currency traders are not blamed for the damage done to these economic tigers. The blame is put squarely on the shoulders of the governments. They are accused of corruption, of cronyism and nepotism, of lack of transparency and generally of bad governance.

For as long as there is this refusal to admit that it was currency trading and the greed of the currency traders which caused the unnecessary destruction of the economies of many countries, for so long will the damage continue to be done to even healthy economies by currency trading. Even the powerful countries will not be free from the threat as the failure of the LTCM Fund demonstrated.

There is no hope that currency trading will be banned or even curbed any time soon. Too many influential people are making too much money from it. That the currency is coming from the misery of poor people in poor countries is just unfortunate.

As one Frenchman said, the genie has been let out of the bottle and no one "in the world" can put it back in. This is a remarkable admission considering that the people who let out the genie are the same people who have appointed themselves as the policemen of the world, the champions of human rights and justice for the oppressed people in the world. The poor and the weak should take note. They are less important than the currency traders, whose freedom must be upheld at all cost.

Malaysia's experience in handling the economic and financial turmoil will stand it in good stead for future turmoils and crises. The most important lesson learnt from the experience is the need to know the true causes of the downturn, how they work and the interrelationship between different factors. Once the details become known, it will be possible to design a strategy to combat the forces causing the problem. Several solutions may present themselves for any one problem, and these solutions need to be debated and tried out. Back-up solutions must be ready should the chosen method fail. The implementation of a strategy or solution requires hands-on monitoring by the decisionmakers, at least in overseeing the implementation process and in taking corrective action.

Complete and continuous information on what is happening on the ground is absolutely essential. Figures, graphs and charts tell a better story than wordy reports. Explanations must be made orally by those reporting. Of course, those getting the reports must be sufficiently knowledgeable on the subjects to be able to make assessments and to decide on what courses of action need to be taken. The system is important but the people working the system are more important. In fact, a good system by itself will only deliver partial solutions at best. The people manning the system are the ones who make the system work.

An important lesson learnt is that Malaysia must always be careful in the management of its economy. It must never allow itself to be weakened by carelessness in the maintenance of its financial and economic strength. Only with absolute vigilance can we ensure that Malaysia's rate of growth will be sufficient to achieve developed country status as envisaged in Vision 2020.

The currency crisis is an unnecessary crisis and need not have happened if the objective of the international financial system is really to facilitate trade and other economic interactions between nations, including FDIs. But the big capitalist powers want more than that. They want to promote their political agenda as well, and it is because of this political agenda that the international financial system not only permitted but at times even encouraged currency trading, a totally unnecessary activity, which destroys more wealth than it creates.

INDEX

ABOUT THE AUTHOR

DR MAHATHIR MOHAMAD, one of the most durable and outspoken figures on the world political stage, has been prime minister of Malaysia since July 16, 1981. He first came to prominence in 1969 when he was expelled from the ruling party, Umno, for writing a letter critical of the then prime minister, Tunku Abdul Rahman. Before being readmitted to Umno in 1972, he wrote his famous, highly controversial work, *The Malay Dilemma* (1970), which examined the economic backwardness of the Malays, and advocated the intervention of the state to bring about their rehabilitation. The book was promptly banned in Malaysia. In his recent books, *The Way Forward* and *A New Deal for Asia*, Dr Mahathir reflects on Malaysia's fight for independence and rails against those who blindly worship the free market.

As Malaysia's fourth prime minister, Dr Mahathir has played a pivotal role in the confident march of his people towards Vision 2020, his blueprint for Malaysia's advance towards fully developed status. Born in 1925, Dr Mahathir studied medicine in Singapore, where he met his future wife, Dr Siti Hasmah Mohd Ali. After working as a doctor in government service, he left to set up his own private medical practice in his hometown, Alor Setar. In 1974, he gave that up to concentrate on his political career. Dr Mahathir and his wife have seven children and ten grandchildren.

what they say about
A NEW DEAL FOR ASIA

A NEW DEAL FOR ASIA looks at whether Asia can reinvent itself for the new millennium after the chaos and turmoil of the Asian crisis. According to Dr Mahathir Mohamad, now is not the time for recriminations, but to reexamine the way the global economic system functions. Now is also the time to look ahead, move on and try to focus on the future again. None of these, however, can be done in isolation. The lesson we must learn from the crisis is that we all share a common fate, and that there must now be a willingness to challenge some of the most fundamental tenets of global capitalism. This book also reflects on the major themes in Dr Mahathir's political agenda. As the architect and strategist of modern Malaysia's phenomenal growth and development over the last quarter of the 20th century, Dr Mahathir seems to thrive on unfashionable ideas, controversial policies and a contentious diplomacy: an enigma baffling to both his detractors and supporters alike.

A NEW DEAL FOR ASIA is as thought-provoking as Dr Mahathir's highly controversial *The Malay Dilemma*, *The Challenge* and *The Way Forward*, all of special interest today as he is at the helm of a nation striving for racial balance and religious sanity.

ISBN 967 978 697 8

THE SUN, MAY 8, 1999

"... Dr Mahathir Mohamad's *A New Deal for Asia* is a very practical book. It shows a practical man with practical ideas applicable not just for Asia but for the rest of the world."

DATO' SERI ABDULLAH AHMAD BADAWI
DEPUTY PRIME MINISTER, MALAYSIA, MAY 24, 1999

"The proposals in the book could be compared to the famous interwar [June 16, 1933] New Deal of US President Franklin D. Roosevelt, which essentially transformed the US, giving hope and actual progress, cutting across racial and economic lines."

THE STAR, JUNE 6, 1999

"As we pick up the pieces, Dr Mahathir's book is timely reading. Those of us who did not want to hear him speak up at that time for fear of further fluctuation in the value of the ringgit, would appreciate his reasoning now."

ASIAWEEK, JULY 23, 1999

"... a chastening read ... Dr Mahathir says much that needs to be said. ... [He] is about the only leader of a democratic, developing country who has the mettle to contradict the big powers. Where others waffle, he cuts to the quick. ... He says publicly what many leaders think, but don't have the guts to enunciate. ... The book's strength is the long section dealing with Malaysia's seemingly inexorable rise during the 1980s and 1990s—and its abrupt fall due to the Crisis. And he is largely right. Indeed, the evidence for his argument grows as time passes. His attacks on the IMF were initially ridiculed as the rantings of a man who was a few sandwiches short of a full picnic.Then others began to echo his criticisms, until the IMF acknowledged a 'slight mistake'. ... he is worth listening to and he does provoke. The prime minister's capacity for provocation is perhaps his greatest attribute."

FAR EASTERN ECONOMIC REVIEW, JUNE 17, 1999

"For those who vehemently opposed to Malaysian Prime Minister Mahathir Mohamad's world view, don't expect his book to be any sort of deviation. For those who consider his anti-Western convictions vindicated by the Asian economic crisis, *A New Deal for Asia* offers a timely and readable reaffirmation. ... What comes through loud and clear is Mahathir's utter dismay at the power of global economic sentiment, and his unflinching belief that Malaysia and the rest of Asia are victims of a new form of imperialism."

MEN'S REVIEW, SEPTEMBER 1999

"... we should seek truth from experience, and as we can't always trust the filters of either the local or foreign press, I would recommend that Dr Mahathir's *A New Deal for Asia* is worth picking up."